Calm Your Mind

First published in the United Kingdom in 2024 by

Batsford

43 Great Ormond Street

London WC1N 3HZ

An imprint of B. T. Batsford Holdings Limited

ISBN 978 1 84994 926 2

A CIP catalogue record for this book is available from the British Library.

10 9 8 7 6 5 4 3 2 1

Reproduction by Mission Productions Ltd, Hong Kong

Printed and bound by Dream Colour, China

This book can be ordered direct from the publisher at www.batsfordbooks.com and www.ravenousbutterflies.com or try your local bookshop.

Ravenous®
Butterflies

Calm Your Mind

BATSFORD

Odilon Redon,
Ophelia among the Flowers, 1905–1908

5

The journey finder

Travel through your emotional innerscape; explore places and feelings along the way using this useful 'journey finder'. Simply match the emotion to the page number. You never know where you might land, or what you'll discover along the way.

ACCEPTANCE
18–19, 132–133

AWE
22–23, 34–35, 48–49,
58–59

GRATITUDE
12–13, 72–73, 90–91

HOPE
44–45, 74–75, 96–97,
136–137

LOVE
32–33, 38–39, 68–69,
104–105, 140–141,
148–149, 158–159,
162–163

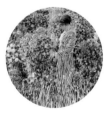

NATURE
22–23, 36–37, 64–65,
118–119, 168–169

🦋

BECOMING
24—25, 52—53, 76—77,
108—109, 122—123,
126—127

🦋

CALM
56—57, 112—115,
138—139, 164—165,
170—171

🦋

COURAGE
26—27, 46—49,
106—107, 124—125

🦋

FRIENDSHIP
62—63, 78—79, 134—135

🦋

INSPIRATION
30—31, 34—35, 60—61,
100—101, 144—145,
166—167

🦋

JOY
58—59, 80—81, 102—103,
142—143

🦋

KINDNESS
16—17, 50—51, 120—121,
150—151, 154—155

🦋

LOSS
54—55, 66—67, 84—85,
116—117, 130—131,
152—153

🦋

OPTIMISM
28—29, 70—71, 86—87,
110—111

🦋

SELF-LOVE
42—43, 82—83, 88—89,
98—99, 128—129,
160—161

🦋

WELLNESS
20—21, 114—115,
146—147, 156—157

🦋

WISDOM
40—41, 92—93

Welcome to *Calm Your Mind* by Ravenous Butterflies, an exploratory journey to encourage mindfulness through the transformative power of art. At times in my life, 'keep calm and carry on' was my daily mantra. It felt like there was always something or someone to fix, a dilemma to unravel and ominous feelings lurking – until now. I'm sure many of you can relate to this; I'm here to reassure you that life does move on, and one day, you'll look back and see how far you or those around you have come. Thankfully, I've moved on, and my fears have shifted; I've found a place of inner peace and absolute calm.

A couple of decades ago, I was morbidly obese and put my life at risk and everything else on the back burner. I had to disconnect myself from myself to survive, and each day was a monumental struggle. It felt as though my head was tethered to my neck by a long string, like a balloon floating aimlessly over my vast body. I couldn't walk without crutches and used a wheelchair; people would poke fun at me or turn away; I was enormously invisible. Life is unbearably hard when you're that size; you don't fit into clothes, chairs don't fit around you and I felt I didn't fit in. How and why did I get into that state? That's a long story for another time, but I'm better than ever now. My children have their mother back, and thankfully, my head is firmly reattached to the rest of me!

Today, I'm grounded, centred and connected to what is important. I'm grateful to the therapy that helped rewire my thoughts and belief systems; it gave me a deluxe toolbox equipped with better skills. The tools I cherish most are love and self-worth; they are the root of confidence, courage and forgiveness. I've learned to own my decision-making and take full responsibility for it. The blame game is pointless; you can't fix what you don't face.

James Jebusa Shannon,
The Purple Stocking, c.1894

These experiences have been a gift; I'm determined to pay it forward. When you face your mortality, it's surprising how sharply things come into focus. Sure, I've faced many difficulties along the way, with divorce, bereavement and much more. But I'm a person whose cup is always half full, and these experiences have made me who I am and given me unique objectives and vigour to succeed, even at my age! I wish I could time travel and reassure my younger self (and my children) that everything works out how it is meant to in the end. The lessons I learned from those bleak years were extreme, but they have enabled me to cherish the good days and made them all the sweeter.

In the process of becoming me, I've shed half my body weight, along with countless tears, sweat and layers of skin. With each new skin, I have become a more whole, self-determining and defined woman.

Throughout all of this, the one thing that has shined on consistently in my life is my love of the arts. Art and books have been my refuge and healing balm in the darkest times. Whenever the world became too cruel for me, I'd take myself off to a gallery or curl up and read or write. Having graduated in art, painting is my happy place, and I'm delighted that my children have become wonderful artists and creatives, too. When they were young, I couldn't play sports with them, so we'd sit around the kitchen table, and I'd draw whatever they wanted so they could colour in and get the glue and glitter out! Invariably, they asked for princesses, fairies and mermaids; they are adults now, and nothing much has changed! We would always make up a story to accompany the characters or play music, such warm memories.

Today, my children are adults, and all four of us access art to improve our mood and help our mental health. I get immense joy visiting galleries and museums with them; what better way to calm your mind and nurture love than to immerse yourself in the beauty of art with your children?

I'm confident this will continue for generations; it's part of our DNA. John Keats defines this with such grace in his poem 'Endymion' (1818).

> A thing of beauty is a joy for ever:
> Its loveliness increases; it will never
> Pass into nothingness; but still will keep
> A bower quiet for us, and a sleep
> Full of sweet dreams, and health, and quiet breathing.

Finding a sense of calm in the maelstrom of life is a necessary antidote. Escaping for a few moments each day and immersing myself in the beauty of art has saved my life. It has given me the ability to think and see more clearly and take time to enjoy simple pleasures. We don't have to run around at a million miles an hour; we can make defined choices to improve our lives when we are calm. The benefit to our physical health is tangible, too.

I'm as fearless as I can be now, but not as fearless as I will become. There is so much to look forward to and much potential to achieve as I glide into my autumn years. Age is a remarkable thing; I've finally grown into the person I always knew I could be, which is wonderfully liberating!

You, too, can find inner calm through art and literature. So, take a deep breath, snuggle down and turn off to the outside world; this is your special space to enrich your life and Calm Your Mind.

Relax and breathe…
This is for you,

Love always,
Lisa Azarmi,
founder of Ravenous Butterflies

'Touch the earth, love the earth, honour the earth, her plains, her valleys, her hills, and her seas; rest your spirit in her solitary places. For the gifts of life are the earth's and they are given to all, and they are the songs of birds at daybreak, Orion and the Bear, and dawn seen over ocean from the beach.'

Henry Beston, from *The Outermost House* (1928)

Frank Dicksee,
On the Brittany Coast

'When I got to the library I came to a standstill, —
ah, the dear room, what happy times I have spent
in it rummaging amongst the books, making plans
for my garden, building castles in the air, writing,
dreaming, doing nothing.'

Elizabeth von Arnim, from *Elizabeth and Her German Garden* (1898)

Félix Vallotton,
The Library, 1921

'Shall we make a new rule of life from tonight: always try to be a little kinder than is necessary?'

J.M. Barrie, from *The Little White Bird* (1902)

Edwin Harris,
Sweet Dreams, 1892

'I drank of the darkness, I was fed with
the honey of fragrance,

I was glad of my life, the drawing of
breath was sweet;

I heard your voice, you said, 'Look down,
see the glow-worm!'

It was there before me, a small star white
at my feet.'

Sara Teasdale, 'August Night',
from *Dark of the Moon* (1926)

Constant Montald,
Dancing Nymphs, 1898

'Doing those deeply unfashionable things — slowing down, letting your spare time expand, getting enough sleep, resting — is a radical act now, but it is essential. This is a crossroads we all know, a moment when you need to shed a skin. If you do, you'll expose all those painful nerve endings and feel so raw that you'll need to take care of yourself for a while. If you don't, then that skin will harden around you.'

Katherine May, from *Wintering: The Power of Rest and Retreat in Difficult Times* (2020)

Gustaf Fjæstad,
Frost in Sunshine, 1921

'She walks in the loveliness she made,
Between the apple-blossom and the water—
She walks among the patterned pied brocade,
Each flower her son, and every tree her daughter.'

Vita Sackville-West, from *The Land* (1926)

Frederick Carl Frieseke,
Lady in a Garden, c.1912

'She was becoming herself and daily casting aside that fictitious self which we assume like a garment with which to appear before the world.'

Kate Chopin, from *The Awakening* (1899)

Félix Vallotton,
Martiniquaise, 1915

'I too am not a bit tamed, I too am untranslatable,
I sound my barbaric yawp over the roofs of the world.'

Walt Whitman, from 'Song of Myself' (1855)

Ellen Thesleff,
Echo, 1891

'Optimism is the faith that leads
to achievement; nothing can be
done without hope.'

Helen Keller, from *Optimism* (1903)

Carl Holsøe,
A Woman Seated at a Table by a Window, c.1900

'Be soft. Do not let the world make you hard. Do not let the pain make you hate. Do not let the bitterness steal your sweetness. Take pride that even though the rest of the world may disagree, you still believe it to be a beautiful place.'

Iain Thomas, from *I Wrote This For You* (2007–17)

Anders Andersen-Lundby,
A Winter's Day with Trees Illuminated by the Sunset, 1887–97

'To love at all is to be vulnerable. Love anything and your heart will be wrung and possibly broken. If you want to make sure of keeping it intact you must give it to no one, not even an animal. Wrap it carefully round with hobbies and little luxuries; avoid all entanglements. Lock it up safe in the casket or coffin of your selfishness. But in that casket, safe, dark, motionless, airless, it will change. It will not be broken; it will become unbreakable, impenetrable, irredeemable. To love is to be vulnerable.'

C.S. Lewis, from *The Four Loves* (1960)

Marie-Guillemine Benoist,
Portrait of Madeleine, 1800

'Light, my light, the world-filling light, the eye-
kissing light, heart-sweetening light!
Ah, the light dances, my darling, at the centre of
my life; the light strikes, my darling, the chords
of my love; the sky opens, the wind runs wild,
laughter passes over the earth.
The butterflies spread their sails on the sea of
light. Lilies and jasmines surge up on the crest
of the waves of light.'

Rabindranath Tagore, from *Gitanjali* (1910)

Emile Claus,
Sunset over Waterloo Bridge, 1916

'I like trees because they seem more resigned to the way they have to live than other things do. I feel as if this tree knows everything I ever think of when I sit here. When I come back to it, I never have to remind it of anything; I begin just where I left off.'

Willa Cather, from *O Pioneers!* (1913)

Franklin Carmichael,
Autumn Hillside, 1920

'A letter is a soul, so faithful an echo of the speaking voice that to the sensitive it is among the richest treasures of love.'

Honoré de Balzac, from *Le Père Goriot* (1835)

Christian Krohg,
Oda with Lamp

'The years have touched her only to enrich her; the flower of her youth had not faded; it only hung more quietly on its stem.'

Henry James,
from *The Portrait of a Lady* (1881)

Peder Mørk Mønsted,
An Old Woman Knitting at the Window, 1929

'The appearance of things changes according
to the emotions; and thus we see magic and
beauty in them, while the magic and beauty
are really in ourselves.'

Kahlil Gibran, from *The Broken Wings* (1912)

Maxfield Parrish,
Ecstasy, 1929

'Believe in a love that is being stored up for you like an inheritance, and have faith that in this love there is a strength and a blessing so large that you can travel as far as you wish without having to step outside it.'

Rainer Maria Rilke, from *Letters to a Young Poet* (1929)

Edward Henry Potthast,
Dutch Interior, 1890

'And once the storm is over, you won't remember how you made it through, how you managed to survive. You won't even be sure, whether the storm is really over. But one thing is certain. When you come out of the storm, you won't be the same person who walked in. That's what this storm's all about.'

Haruki Murakami, from *Kafka on the Shore* (2002)

Nikolay Nikanorovich Dubovskoy,
It Grew Quiet, 1890

'Dwell on the beauty of life. Watch the stars,
and see yourself running with them.'

Marcus Aurelius, from *Meditations* (c.161–180 CE)

Thure Sundell,
Moonlight

'Had I the heavens' embroidered cloths,
Enwrought with golden and silver light,
The blue and the dim and the dark cloths
Of night and light and the half light,
I would spread the cloths under your feet:
But I, being poor, have only my dreams;
I have spread my dreams under your feet;
Tread softly because you tread on my dreams.'

W. B. Yeats, 'Aedh Wishes for the Cloths of Heaven',
from *The Wind Among the Reeds* (1899)

Edward Robert Hughes,
Twilight Fantasies, 1911

'...your vision will become clear only when you can look into your own heart... Who looks outside dreams; who looks inside awakes.'

Carl Jung, from letter to Fanny Bowditch,
22 October 1916

Jens Ferdinand Willumsen,
Young Woman Walking in the Mountains, 1904

'It's so curious: one can resist tears and
"behave" very well in the hardest hours of
grief. But then someone makes you a friendly
sign behind a window, or one notices that a
flower that was in bud only yesterday has
suddenly blossomed, or a letter slips from a
drawer... and everything collapses.'

Colette (1873–1954)

Leon Wyczółkowski,
Gościeradza, 1933

'I will be calm.
I will be mistress of myself.'

Jane Austen, from *Sense and Sensibility* (1811)

Harald Slott-Møller,
Midsummer's Eve, 1904

'I love the sensual.
For me this
and love for the sun
has a share in brilliance and beauty.'

Sappho, from *Poems of Sappho*,
translated by Julia Dubnoff

Olga Kurtz Hasselmann,
Josephine Baker, c.1930

'Out beyond ideas of wrongdoing
and rightdoing there is a field.
I'll meet you there.

When the soul lies down in that grass
the world is too full to talk about.'

Rumi, from 'A Great Wagon'

Janet Fisher,
Distant Thoughts

'Old friends become more and more precious to us as the years pass. They can look at us for who we once were and who we are now, appreciating the difficulties we have overcome, the abilities we have acquired, and the ways we have stayed true to ourselves.'

Wendy Lustbader, from *Life Gets Better: The Unexpected Pleasures of Growing Older* (2011)

Michael Ancher,
Promenade on the Beach

'Live in each season as it passes; breathe the air, drink the drink, taste the fruit, and resign yourself to the influences of each.'

Henry David Thoreau, *Journal* (August 23, 1853)

William Fraser Garden,
A Great Tree on a Riverbank, 1892

'...and, when he shall die,
Take him and cut him out in little stars,
And he will make the face of heaven so fine
That all the world will be in love with night
And pay no worship to the garish sun.'

William Shakespeare, from *Romeo and Juliet* (1597–99)

Edwin Howland Blashfield,
Spring Scattered Stars, 1927

'Love me, sweet, with all thou art,
Feeling, thinking, seeing,—
Love me in the lightest part,
Love me in full being.'

Elizabeth Barrett Browning,
from 'A Man's Requirements' (1841)

Paul Ranson,
The Blue or Nude Room at the Fan, 1891

'Let me imagine that we will come again
when we want to and it will be spring
we will be no older than we ever were
the worn griefs will have eased like the early cloud
through which the morning slowly comes to itself
and the ancient defenses against the dead
will be done with and left to the dead at last
the light will be as it is now in the garden
that we have made here these years together
of our long evenings and astonishment'

W. S. Merwin, 'To Paula in Late Spring', from *The Shadow of Sirius* (2009)

Nikolai Astrup,
March Morning, Spring Night and Willow

Martzmorgen
N. Astrup

'Well, He had known what love was-a
sharp pang, a fierce experience, in the
midst of whose flames he was struggling!
But, through that furnace he would fight
his way out into the serenity of middle
age,-all the richer and more human for
having known this great passion.'

Elizabeth Gaskell, from *North and South* (1854)

Edvard Munch,
The Kiss, 1892

'"Hope" is the thing with feathers
That perches is in the soul,
And sings the tune without the words,
And never stops at all...'

Emily Dickinson, from '"Hope" is the Thing with Feathers'
(c.1858–62)

Gaston La Touche,
Lovers and Swans; The Autumn Walk, 1896

'Live! Live the wonderful life that is in you! Let nothing be lost upon you. Be always searching for new sensations. Be afraid of nothing.'

Oscar Wilde, from *The Picture of Dorian Gray* (1890)

Henry Scott Tuke,
The Critics, 1927

'The glory of friendship is not the outstretched hand, nor the kindly smile, nor the joy of companionship; it is the spiritual inspiration that comes to one when you discover that someone else believes in you and is willing to trust you with a friendship.'

Ralph Waldo Emerson (1803–82)

Peder Severin Krøyer,
Hip Hip Hurrah! Artists' Party at Skagen, 1888

'A thing of beauty is a joy for ever:
Its loveliness increases; it will never
Pass into nothingness; but still will keep
A bower quiet for us, and a sleep
Full of sweet dreams, and health, and quiet breathing.'

John Keats, 'Endymion' (1818)

Pierre Bonnard,
The Garden under the Snow, Sunset, c.1910

'Now you understand
Just why my head's not bowed.
I don't shout or jump about
Or have to talk real loud.
When you see me passing,
It ought to make you proud.
I say,
It's in the click of my heels,
The bend of my hair,
the palm of my hand,
The need for my care.
'Cause I'm a woman
Phenomenally.
Phenomenal woman,
That's me.'

Maya Angelou, from 'Phenomenal Woman' (1978)

Augustus John,
Head of a Jamaican Girl, c.1937

'It isn't possible to love and to part.
You will wish that it was. You can
transmute love, ignore it, muddle it,
but you can never pull it out of you.
I know by experience that the poets
are right: love is eternal.'

E.M. Forster, from *A Room with a View* (1908)

Lawrence Alma-Tadema,
The Favourite Poet, 1888

'Let us bring up our children. It is not the place of some official to hand to them their heritage.

If others impart to our children our knowledge and ideals, they will lose all of us that is wordless and full of wonder.

Let us build memories in our children,

lest they drag out joyless lives,

lest they allow treasures to be lost because

they have not been given the keys.

We live, not by things, but by the meanings of things.

It is needful to transmit the passwords from generation to generation.'

Antoine de Saint-Exupéry, from 'Generation to Generation'

Jules Bastien-Lepage,
Le Père Jacques (The Wood Gatherer), 1881

'Winter is the time for comfort, for good food and warmth, for the touch of a friendly hand and for a talk beside the fire: it is the time for home.'

Edith Sitwell (1887–1964)

Angus Hampel,
Hope, 2015

'There is within each one of us a potential for goodness beyond our imagining; for giving which seeks no reward; for listening without judgment; for loving unconditionally. There are no mistakes, no coincidences. All events are blessings given to us to learn from.'

Elisabeth Kübler-Ross (1926–2004)

Frank Bramley,
Eyes and No Eyes, 1887

'We're all just walking each other home.'

Ram Dass (1931–2019)

Hugo Simberg,
Towards the Evening, 1913

'True happiness is to enjoy the present, without anxious dependence upon the future, not to amuse ourselves with either hopes or fears but to rest satisfied with what we have, which is sufficient, for he that is so wants nothing. The greatest blessings of mankind are within us and within our reach. A wise man is content with his lot, whatever it may be, without wishing for what he has not.'

Seneca (c.1 BCE–CE 65)

Firmin Baes,
The Dream of the Lacemaker

'It was November — the month of crimson sunsets, parting birds, deep, sad hymns of the sea, passionate wind-songs in the pines. Anne roamed through the pineland alleys in the park and let that great sweeping wind blow the fogs out of her soul.'

L.M. Montgomery, from *Anne of the Island* (1915)

Childe Hassam,
Rain Storm, Union Square, 1890

'Difficult times have helped me to understand better than before, how infinitely rich and beautiful life is in every way, and that so many things that one goes worrying about are of no importance whatsoever.'

Isak Dinesen (1885–1962)

'But there is an influence in the light of the morning that tends to rectify whatever errors of fancy, or even of judgment, we may have incurred during the sun's decline, or among the shadows of the night, or in the less wholesome glow of moonshine.'

Nathaniel Hawthorne, from *Rappaccini's Daughter* (1844)

Lamorna Birch,
The Dipper's Playground, 1948

'Now and then, it's good
to pause in our pursuit of
happiness and just be happy.'

Guillaume Apollinaire (1880–1918)

'I love you not only for what you are, but for what I am when I am with you. I love you not only for what you have made of yourself, but for what you are making of me. I love you for the part of me that you bring out.'

Elizabeth Barrett Browning (1806–1861)

Jules Bastien-Lepage,
Rural Love, 1882

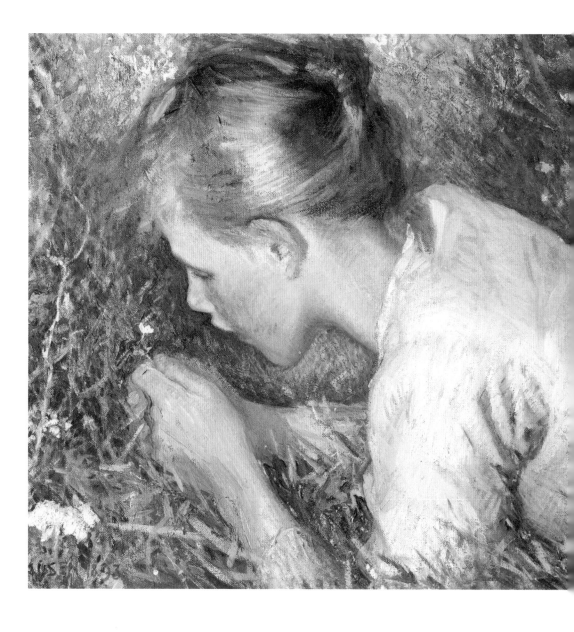

'Magic is believing in yourself, if
you can do that, you can make
anything happen.'

Johann Wolfgang von Goethe (1749–1832)

George Clausen,
The Little Flowers of the Field, 1895

'Only a few, who remain children at heart, can ever find that fair, lost path again; and blessed are they above mortals. They, and only they, can bring us tidings from that dear country where we once sojourned and from which we must evermore be exiles. The world calls them its singers and poets and artists and story-tellers; but they are just people who have never forgotten the way to fairyland.'

L.M. Montgomery, from *The Story Girl* (1911)

Nikolai Astrup,
Foxgloves, woodblock c.1915–20; print 1925

'Life will break you. Nobody can protect you from that. And living alone won't either, for solitude will also break you with its yearning. You have to love. You have to feel. It is the reason you are here on Earth.'

Louise Erdrich, from *The Painted Drum* (2005)

Marie Bashkirtseff,
The Umbrella, 1883

'Reading is escape, and the opposite of escape; it's a way to make contact with reality after a day of making things up, and it's a way of making contact with someone else's imagination after a day that's all too real.'

Nora Ephron, from *I Feel Bad About My Neck* (2006)

Henri Lebasque,
Girl Reading

'I love to watch the fine mist of the night come on,
The windows and the stars illumined, one by one,
The rivers of dark smoke pour upward lazily,
And the moon rise and turn them silver. I shall see
The springs, the summers, and the autumns slowly pass;
And when old Winter puts his blank face to the glass,
I shall close all my shutters, pull the curtains tight,
And build me stately palaces by candlelight.'

Charles Baudelaire, from *Les Fleurs du Mal* (1857)

Harald Oskar Sohlberg,
Winter Nights in the Mountains, 1914

'Deep in her soul, however, she was waiting for something to happen. Like a sailor in distress, she would gaze out over the solitude of her life with desperate eyes, seeking some white sail in the mists of the far-off horizon. She did not know what this chance event would be, what wind would drive it to her, what shore it would carry her to.'

Gustave Flaubert, from *Madame Bovary* (1856)

Laura Knight,
Lamorna Cove, c.1912

'Yes, I love it!... The sea is only the embodiment of a supernatural and wonderful existence. It is nothing but love and emotion; it is the "Living Infinite", as one of your poets has said.'

Jules Verne, from *Twenty Thousand Leagues Under the Sea* (1870)

John William Waterhouse,
A Mermaid, 1900

'A sensitive plant in a garden grew,
And the young winds fed it with silver dew,
And it opened its fan-like leaves to the light,
And closed them beneath the kisses of Night.

And the Spring arose on the garden fair,
Like the Spirit of Love felt everywhere;
And each flower and herb on Earth's dark breast
Rose from the dreams of its wintry rest.

But none ever trembled and panted with bliss
In the garden, the field, or the wilderness,
Like a doe in the noontide with love's sweet want,
As the companionless Sensitive Plant.'

Percy Bysshe Shelley, 'The Sensitive Plant' (1820)

Frank Dicksee,
The Sensitive Plant

'The woman who first gives life, light, and form to our shadowy conceptions of beauty, fills a void in our spiritual nature that has remained unknown to us till she appeared... The mystery which underlies the beauty of women is never raised above the reach of all expression until it has claimed kindred with the deeper mystery in our own souls.'

Wilkie Collins, from *The Woman in White* (1860)

Pierre Bonnard, *Nude in Backlighting*
or *The Eau de Cologne*, 1908–9

'I know what I want, I have a goal, an opinion, I have a religion and love. Let me be myself and then I am satisfied. I know that I'm a woman, a woman with inward strength and plenty of courage.'

Anne Frank, from *The Diary of a Young Girl* (1947)

Edward Atkinson Hornel,
Tom-Tom Players, Ceylon, 1908

'I wanted to change the world. But I have found that the only thing one can be sure of changing is oneself.'

Aldous Huxley, from *Point Counter Point* (1928)

George Henry and Edward Atkinson Hornel,
The Druids: Bringing in the Mistletoe, 1890

'I can live alone, if self-respect, and circumstances require me so to do. I need not sell my soul to buy bliss. I have an inward treasure born with me, which can keep me alive if all extraneous delights should be withheld, or offered only at a price I cannot afford to give.'

Charlotte Brontë, from *Jane Eyre* (1847)

Pekka Halonen,
Woman in Boat, 1924

'Don't be ashamed to weep; 'tis right to grieve.
Tears are only water, and flowers, trees, and
fruit cannot grow without water. But there
must be sunlight also. A wounded heart will
heal in time, and when it does, the memory
and love of our lost ones is sealed inside to
comfort us.'

Brian Jacques, from *The Taggerung* (2001)

Dod Procter,
Gabriel in St Lucia, c.1950s

'Never regret anything you have done with a sincere affection; nothing is lost that is born of the heart.'

Basil Rathbone (1892–1967)

Peter Ilsted,
The Open Door, 1912

'When we honestly ask ourselves which person in our lives mean the most to us, we often find that it is those who, instead of giving advice, solutions, or cures, have chosen rather to share our pain and touch our wounds with a warm and tender hand. The friend who can be silent with us in a moment of despair or confusion, who can stay with us in an hour of grief and bereavement, who can tolerate not knowing, not curing, not healing and face with us the reality of our powerlessness, that is a friend who cares.'

Henri Nouwen, from *Out of Solitude* (1974)

Richard E. Miller,
Afternoon Tea, 1910

'Yet if hope has flown away
In a night, or in a day,
In a vision, or in none,
Is it therefore the less *gone?*
All that we see or seem
Is but a dream within a dream.'

Edgar Allan Poe, 'A Dream Within a Dream' (1849)

Eilif Peterssen,
Nocturne, 1887

'There are two ways of seeing: with the body and with the soul. The body's sight can sometimes forget, but the soul remembers forever.'

Alexandre Dumas, from *The Count of Monte Cristo* (1844–6)

Gustav Klimt,
Island in the Attersee, 1902

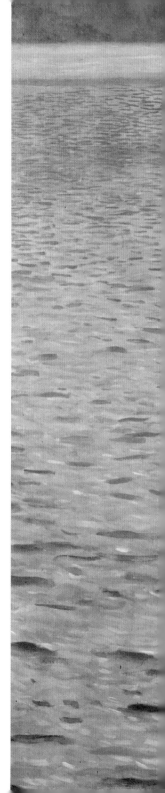

'To love or have loved, that is enough. Ask nothing further.
There is no other pearl to be found in the dark folds of life.'

Victor Hugo, from *Les Misérables* (1862)

Marc Chagall,
Bouquet with Flying Lovers, c.1934–47

'Enjoy the little things, for one
day you may look back and
realise they were the big things.'

Robert Brault, in *National Enquirer* (1985)

Christian Krohg,
Little Ebbe Reading, 1920

'Keep some room in your heart for the unimaginable.'

Mary Oliver, from *Evidence* (2009)

Hovsep Pushman,
The Incense Burner, c.1919

'Nobody has ever measured,
not even poets, how much
the heart can hold.'

Zelda Fitzgerald (1900 – 1948)

František Dvořák,
The Angel of the Birds, 1910

'They looked at each other and laughed, then looked away, filled with darkness and secrecy. Then they kissed and remembered the magnificence of the night. It was so magnificent, such an inheritance of a universe of dark reality, that they were afraid to seem to remember. They hid away the remembrance and the knowledge.'

D.H. Lawrence, from *Women in Love* (1920)

Winslow Homer,
A Summer Night, 1890

'How it is that animals understand things I do not know, but it is certain that they do understand. Perhaps there is a language which is not made of words and everything in the world understands it. Perhaps there is a soul hidden in everything and it can always speak, without even making a sound, to another soul.'

Frances Hodgson Burnett, from *A Little Princess* (1905)

Peder Severin Krøyer, *Summer Evening at Skagen, the Artist's Wife with a Dog on the Beach*, 1892

'Everything about her was warm and soft and scented; even the stains of her grief became her as raindrops do the beaten rose.'

Edith Wharton, from *The House of Mirth* (1905)

John William Waterhouse,
Soul of the Rose, 1908

'Animals are such agreeable
friends — they ask no questions;
they pass no criticisms.'

George Eliot, from 'Mr Gilfil's Love Story'
(1857)

Suzanne Valadon,
Bouquet and a Cat, 1919

'I've dreamt in my life dreams that have stayed with me ever after, and changed my ideas: they've gone through and through me, like wine through water, and altered the colour of my mind.'

Emily Brontë, from *Wuthering Heights* (1847)

Eva Gonzalès,
Woman Awakening, 1876

'I do not love you as if you were salt-rose, or topaz,
or the arrow of carnations the fire shoots off.
I love you as certain dark things are to be loved,
in secret, between the shadow and the soul.

I love you as the plant that never blooms
but carries in itself the light of hidden flowers;
thanks to your love a certain solid fragrance,
risen from the earth, lives darkly in my body.'

Pablo Neruda, 'Sonnet XVII', from *One Hundred Love Sonnets*,
translated by Mark Eisner (1959)

Lawrence Alma-Tadema,
In a Rose Garden

'Be yourself; no base imitator of another, but your best self. There is something which you can do better than another. Listen to the inward voice and bravely obey that. Do the things at which you are great, not what you were never made for.'

Ralph Waldo Emerson, from *Self-Reliance and Other Essays* (1844)

John Lavery,
Anna Pavlova, 1910

'Even this late it happens:
the coming of love, the coming of light.
You wake and the candles are lit as if by themselves,
stars gather, dreams pour into your pillows,
sending up warm bouquets of air.
Even this late the bones of the body shine
and tomorrow's dust flares into breath.'

Mark Strand, from 'The Coming of Light' (1978)

Pierre-Auguste Renoir,
Confidence, 1897

'Blessed are they who see beautiful things in humble places where other people see nothing. The whole world is beautiful, the art is in the seeing. Paint the essential character of things.'

Camille Pissarro (1830–1903)

Camille Pissarro,
Road Climbing to Osny, 1883

'I have always been delighted at
the prospect of a new day, a fresh
try, one more start, with perhaps
a bit of magic waiting somewhere
behind the morning.'

J.B. Priestley (1894–1984)

George Henry,
Japanese Lady with a Fan, 1894

'There is a pleasure in the pathless woods,
There is a rapture on the lonely shore,
There is society where none intrudes,
By the deep Sea, and music in its roar:
I love not Man the less, but Nature more.'

Lord Byron, from *Childe Harold's Pilgrimage* (1812)

Akseli Gallen-Kallela,
Lake Keitele, 1905

'Bring me all of your dreams,
You dreamers,
Bring me all of your
Heart melodies
That I may wrap them
In a blue cloud-cloth
Away from the too-rough fingers
Of the world.'

Langston Hughes, 'The Dream Keeper' (1932)

Utagawa Hiroshige,
New Year's Eve Foxfires at the Changing Tree, Ōji, c.1857

Artist biographies

Sir Lawrence Alma-Tadema
1836–1912, Holland
Romanticism, Academic Art
Sir Lawrence Alma-Tadema trained at the Royal Academy of Antwerp before settling in England in 1870. A painter of lavish classical subjects, he was famous for his depictions of the excesses of the Roman Empire. He was admired for his meticulous attention to detail and draughtsmanship.

Michael Ancher
1849–1927, Denmark
Realism, Skagen School
Michael Ancher was unable to complete his education due to poverty, but he began to draw, capturing the essence of the long midsummer evenings. In 1871 he was accepted at the Royal Danish Academy of Fine Arts in Copenhagen. This is where he met Karl Madsen who prompted him to go to Skagen. Ancher's paintings of the fishing community, the Skagerak and the North Sea brought him notoriety.

Anders Andersen-Lundby
1841–1923, Denmark
Landscapes
Anders Andersen-Lundby was mostly known for his realistic paintings of winter landscapes in Denmark and Southern Germany. His first major exhibition was in Copenhagen, where he gained much popularity. In 1865, he married Thora Adelheid Børgesen.

Nikolai Astrup
1880–1928, Norway
Modernism, Neo-Romanticism, Symbolism
Nikolai Astrup was the son of a pastor and the eldest of fourteen children. Astrup's father wanted him to join the priesthood, but he did not excel in school; he enjoyed painting and handwork instead. He spent much of his time outdoors painting, and in 1899, he moved to Oslo and spent two weeks learning printmaking at the Royal Drawing School. He later studied at Harriet Backer's School of Painting, before moving to Paris, where he studied under Christian Krohg at the Académie Colarossi.

Firmin Baes
1874–1943, Belgium
Realism, pastels, printmaker
Firmin Baes was raised in a family of artists. He worked with his father, painting decorative panels in homes and hotels in Brussels. He met the painter Léon Frédéric, who became his tutor, and in 1888, he enrolled at the Académie Royale des Beaux-Arts in Brussels. Together with some people who worked with his father, Baes developed a pastel technique using canvas, which brought a soft, velvety feel to the drawings and an added tenderness to the subject matter.

Marie Bashkirtseff
1858–1884, Ukraine
Diarist, painter, sculptor, Realism, Naturalism

Marie Bashkirtseff was born into Russian nobility in present-day Ukraine. She grew up travelling with her mother through Europe, eventually settling in Paris. She was determined to become a singer, but illness destroyed her voice. She studied painting at the Académie Julien, one of the rare schools to accept women. Bashkirtseff exhibited at the Paris Salon in 1880. She was an active feminist and wrote several articles for Hubertine Auclert's feminist newspaper *La Citoyenne* in 1881 under the pseudonym Pauline Orrel. She died of tuberculosis at the age of twenty-five.

Jules Bastien-Lepage
1848–1884, France
Realism, Naturalism

Jules Bastien-Lepage's parents encouraged him to draw from a young age. He enjoyed painting the apple trees and fruit orchards around his home in northeast France. He studied at the École des Beaux-Arts in 1867 and was tutored by Cabanel. He was hugely influenced by Courbet and Millet and had great success with his paintings, which he exhibited widely. His earthy palette and depictions of rural life greatly influenced the Glasgow Boys.

Marie-Guillemine Benoist
1768–1826, France
Neoclassicism

Marie-Guillemine Benoist studied under Élisabeth Vigée Le Brun. She later studied at the atelier of Jacques-Louis David alongside her sister, Marie-Élisabeth Laville-Leroux. Benoist exhibited and her influence and success continued. She was an advocate for women and set up a studio to teach them. Sadly, she had to abandon painting and women's advocacy due to the political leanings of her husband, Comte Benoist, and the popularity of conservatism in Europe.

Lamorna Birch
1869–1955, Britain
Newlyn School

Samuel John 'Lamorna' Birch was a self-taught artist from Cheshire, England. In the late 1880s, he travelled to Cornwall and was so smitten with Lamorna Cove that he changed his name to Lamorna Birch. Seduced by the clear light and creative environment, he moved to Lamorna Valley in 1892. He has become regarded as a forefather of the Newlyn School of Artists.

Edwin Howland Blashfield
1848–1936, America
Murals

Edwin Howland Blashfield studied engineering at the Massachusetts Institute of Technology before attending the Pennsylvania Academy of Fine Art. In 1867, he moved to Paris and studied academic techniques, exhibiting in many salon shows. He is best known for his murals in high-profile public buildings, including the central dome of the Library of Congress. He received many honours, including a Gold Medal from the American Institute of Architects (1934) and a doctorate from New York University (1926).

Pierre Bonnard
1867–1947, France
Post-Impressionism, Les Nabis
Pierre Bonnard spent much of his childhood drawing and painting in his parent's country garden. Later, he studied law and attended art classes at the Académie Julien in Paris, where he met Paul Sérusier, Maurice Denis and Paul Ranson. Seduced by colour, shimmering light and pattern, the group formed Les Nabis. Bonnard also focused on decorative arts, and was profoundly influenced by Japanese culture. He became an early member of the Art Nouveau movement.

Frank Bramley
1857–1915, Britain
Newlyn School, Post-Impressionist
Frank Bramley attended Lincoln School of Art from 1879–82 and completed his studies at the Royal Academy of Fine Arts in Antwerp. He moved to Newlyn in Cornwall in 1884, where he met and married fellow painter Katherine Graham. Bramley was known for using the square brush technique, which gave the canvas an exciting iridescence and pattern of brushstrokes. His fascination with vibrant light shines through his work. He was a leading figure of the Newlyn School.

Franklin Carmichael
1890–1945, Canada
Group of Seven, illustration
Franklin Carmichael's artistic talents were apparent from a young age. His mother encouraged him to take music and art lessons. His father owned a carriage-making shop; Carmichael practised his design, painting and drawing skills while decorating the carriages. Carmichael is known for using watercolours and his love of the Ontario countryside. He was the youngest member of the Group of Seven and often felt like an outsider. His vivid style and spiritual views were potently expressed through his painting.

Marc Chagall
1887–1985, Belarus/France
Modernism, Symbolism, Expressionism, Surrealism, Fauvism, Cubism
Marc Chagall was deeply influenced by Jewish and Eastern European folklore. He spent the war years in Belarus and founded the Vitebsk Arts College. In 1923, following the Bolshevik Revolution, he left for Paris. He escaped occupied France and fled to New York, where he remained until 1948. Chagall is regarded as the most eminent Jewish artist of the twentieth century and is known worldwide for his stunning stained-glass windows.

Emile Claus
1849–1924, Belgium
Luminism, Expressionism, Impressionism
Emile Claus's father disapproved of his son becoming a painter and sent him to learn to be a baker. With the help of his father's friend, the composer Peter Benoit, Claus persuaded his father to allow him to attend Antwerp Academy of Fine Arts. Claus soon prospered and, influenced by Claude Monet, he developed a style characterised as Luminism. In 1904, he started the artist group Vie et Lumière, 'Life and Light'.

Sir George Clausen
1852–1944, Britain
British Impressionism, British War Art, Rural Naturalism
George Clausen was the son of a decorative painter, his training included a short stint at the Académie Julien in Paris. While in France, he was influenced by the Impressionists and en plein air painting. He studied the effects of changing light and made paintings of figures set against the sun or a shimmering backdrop. He co-founded the New English Art Club in 1886 and was a professor of painting at the Royal Academy from 1904 to 1906. He was knighted in 1927.

Sir Francis 'Frank' Dicksee
1853–1928, Britain
Victorian painter and illustrator
Frank Dicksee was taught painting with his sister, Margaret, by their father, Thomas Dicksee. In 1870, Dicksee began at the Royal Academy Schools, achieving great success. His wistful, allegorical themes were hugely popular; he became president of the RA in 1924. His success continued, and he was knighted in 1925.

Nikolay Nikanorovich Dubovskoy
1859–1918, Russia
Landscape mood, Realism
Nikolay Nikanorovich Dubovskoy was taught to draw from memory at a young age by his uncle. Dubovskoy's father, a troop sergeant, forced his son to join the army cadets. The army instructors soon realised Dubovskoy's artistic talent and persuaded his father to send him to art school instead. Dubovskoy went on to graduate from the Imperial Academy of Art. He was associated with the Peredvizhniki, Russian realist painters, and, along with Isaac Levitan, was instrumental in creating what became known as the 'Landscape of Mood'.

František Dvořák
1862–1927, Czechoslovakia
Art Nouveau, Symbolism
František Dvořák, also known as Franz Dvorak or Franz Bruner, studied at the Munich Academy of Fine Arts. His first solo show took place in Prague in 1907. Dvořák was fascinated with Eastern and New Spirituality, painting several portraits of Ramakrishna and Sarada Devi.

Janet Fisher
1867–1926, Britain
Painter, engraver
Janet Fisher was the daughter of a clergyman. She studied art into her early thirties at Hubert von Herkomer's school in Herefordshire. She learned several printmaking techniques, including mezzotints, etchings and woodcuts.

Gustaf Fjæstad
1868–1948, Sweden
Rackstad Colony, craft, furniture design
Gustaf Fjæstad was an accomplished painter and craftsman; he also assisted Bruno Liljefors at the Biological Museum in Stockholm. Fjæstad mainly painted scenes from nature and is particularly noted for his breath-taking winter landscapes; he also designed furniture, including for the Thielska Gallery. In 1898, he co-founded the Rackstad Colony.

Frederick Carl Frieseke
1874–1939, America
Impressionism
Frederick Carl Frieseke spent most of his life as an expatriate in France; he was an influential member of the Giverny art colony. His work shows his fascination with the effects of dappled sunlight. Most of his work depicts the female form, in harmony with their surroundings.

Akseli Gallen-Kallela
1865–1931, Finland
Romantic nationalism, Realism, Symbolism
Akseli Gallen-Kallela is best known for his illustrations of the *Kalevala*, the Finnish national epic. He captured the wild landscape, changing weather and seasons using a combination of strident and sensitive brushwork.

William Fraser Garden
1856–1921, Scotland
Watercolour, landscapes
William Fraser Garden was born into a family of artists. To stand out from his five brothers, who were all artists, Garden swapped his name around from Garden William Fraser to William Fraser Garden. He was unknown in his lifetime, but his astonishing watercolour technique makes him one of the most remarkable watercolourists in history. Primarily a landscape painter, Garden flooded the paper with light, carefully delineating every blade of grass, branch and twig.

Eva Gonzalès
1849–1883, France
Impressionism
Eva Gonzalès was introduced to intellectuals and artists from an early age by her father, the author Emmanuel Gonzalès. She began art lessons with the painter Charles Chaplin, and became the model and student of Édouard Manet. Gonzalès's work was popular and admired by Salon reviewers, making her one of four eminent female Impressionists.

Pekka Halonen
1865–1933, Finland
Romanticism, Realism
Pekka Halonen's father was an amateur painter and farmer; Halonen accompanied him and assisted with the decorative painting of the interiors of local churches. He studied in Helsinki and won a scholarship to study at the Académie Julien in Paris in 1890. Paul Gauguin was his tutor. He travelled extensively through Europe and studied early Renaissance art. In 1895, he married Maija Mäkinen, and they had eight children.

Angus Hampel
Born 1973, Britain
Modernism
Angus Hampel studied Latin, Greek and Philosophy at Oxford University. He has been painting since joining evening classes in London. He regularly exhibits between Europe and the USA.

Edwin Harris
1855–1906, Britain
Newlyn School
Edwin Harris attended the Birmingham School of Art at fourteen and became an assistant master two years later. Attracted by the clear light in Newlyn, Cornwall and Brittany, he travelled to both areas and enjoyed painting en plein air with his fellow artists. In 1883, Harris settled in Newlyn and became one of the founders of the Newlyn School, which became a foundation for modern painting in Britain.

Childe Hassam
1859–1935, America
American Impressionism
Childe Hassam enjoyed art from an early age. He studied wood engraving and later worked with the engraver George Johnson. Hassam became an illustrator and exhibited his watercolours in his first solo show in Boston. Hassam began painting cityscapes and his paintings continued to sell well. In 1886, he moved to Paris with his wife Maud. There, Hassam joined the prestigious Académie Julien. He took formal drawing classes but found this stifling and soon left; Hassam's painting technique became freer.

Olga Kurtz Hasselmann
1864–1938, Russia
Pastel, painting
Olga Kurtz Hasselmann was known for her use of pastels. She created sensitive, evocative images by applying them in a painterly manner.

George Henry
1858–1943, Scotland
The Glasgow Boys
George Henry studied at Glasgow School of Art and later at Macgregor's studio, learning most from his nature studies in the countryside surrounding Kirkcudbright. Henry became known for his landscapes, folk and Japanese-influenced paintings. He was a member of the Glasgow Boys, and his friendship with Edward Atkinson Hornel led to some exciting collaborative work (see page 126). They were among the first British artists to visit Japan, travelling together in 1893.

Utagawa Hiroshige
1797–1858, Japan
Ukiyo-e
Utagawa Hiroshige was born Andō Tokutarō. Both his parents died when he was fourteen; he found solace in painting. Hiroshige is best known for his horizontal landscape series and views of Edo. He was a master printmaker and painter and considered the last great master of that tradition, but he never had financial security. In 1856, he became a Buddhist monk and died aged sixty-two from the great Edo cholera epidemic of 1858.

Carl Vilhelm Holsøe
1863–1935, Denmark
Realism
Carl Vilhelm Holsøe studied at the Royal Academy in Copenhagen, followed by the Kunstnernes Studieskole under Peder Severin Krøyer, the most highly esteemed Danish artist of the time. Holsøe is recognised for his atmospheric, sparse

interiors, which convey a sense of longing and quiet akin to Johannes Vermeer's Dutch masterpieces.

Winslow Homer
1836–1910, America
American Realism, Tile Club, illustration
Winslow Homer didn't attend formal art institutions; he was taught by his mother, an accomplished watercolourist. He started his career as an apprentice lithographer and illustrator and later set up a successful studio. He travelled to Paris and was influenced by the work of Millet and Courbet. On his return to the US in 1877, Homer exhibited at the Boston Art Club; he also became a member of the Tile Club, where he was known as the 'obtuse bard'. Homer became very reclusive; he lived at Eastern Point Lighthouse for a while, painting the sea and the fishing communities nearby.

Edward Atkinson Hornel
1864–1933, Britain
Landscapes, the Glasgow Boys
Edward Atkinson Hornel, also known as Ned Hornel, was born in Australia to Scottish parents. Hornel moved to Scotland and became a prominent painter; he studied under Charles Verlat in Antwerp after graduating from art school in Edinburgh. Hornel loved travelling and was strongly influenced by the colours and patterns from Japan and the Orient. He was a prominent member of the Glasgow Boys, collaborating with George Henry (see page 126).

Edward Robert Hughes
1851–1914, Britain
Pre-Raphaelite, Aestheticism
Edward Robert Hughes was a painter of extraordinary imagination and skill; his subject matter has strong fantasy elements. Hughes was a vital member of the Pre-Raphaelite Brotherhood. He was also a studio assistant to William Holman Hunt. Hunt suffered from glaucoma, and Hughes substantially contributed to several of Hunt's paintings.

Peter Ilsted
1861–1933, Denmark
Copenhagen Interior School, mezzotints
Peter Ilsted was the brother-in-law of painter Vilhelm Hammershøi. Together with Carl Holsøe, he was known for painting images of 'sunshine and silent rooms'. Ilsted was hugely successful during his lifetime and won many awards. He also made advances with mezzotints, which proved very popular in his day.

Augustus John
1878–1961, Britain
Modernist, printmaker, painting
Augustus John was born in Wales; he was the younger brother of painter Gwen John. He attended Slade School of Art with his sister, Gwen. In 1911, John established an artist's colony at Alderney Manor, Dorset, with his partner Dorelia McNeill. By the 1920s, he was Britain's leading portrait painter.

Gustav Klimt
1862–1918, Austria
Art Nouveau, Vienna Secession, Symbolism, Modern Art
Gustav Klimt won a scholarship to the Vienna School of Arts and Crafts, where his brother also attended. The brothers teamed up with their friend, Franz Matsch, and received several commissions to decorate and paint interiors of prominent buildings; they called themselves the 'Company of Artists'. After graduating, the trio opened a studio specialising in interior decoration, notably theatres. After the death of his brother, Ernst, in 1892, Gustav retreated from public life. Most of Klimt's work is defined by his use of gold, pattern and eroticism; he also made several paintings of gardens, water and his homestead.

Dame Laura Knight
1877–1970, Britain
Impressionism, Newlyn School
Dame Laura Knight was a prolific artist, who designed a poster during World War II for the Women's Land Army. Laura (née Johnson) met Harold Knight at art school; they married in 1903. In late 1907 the Knights moved to Newlyn, Cornwall before settling in the nearby village of Lamorna. Together with Lamorna Birch and Alfred Munnings, they became integral figures in the artist's colony known as the Newlyn School.

Christian Krohg
1852–1925, Norway
Realism, Romanticism, Naturalism
Christian Krohg was a painter, illustrator, author and journalist. He studied art under Hans Gude at the Baden School of Art. Krohg took his inspiration from everyday life and, while working in Paris from 1881–82, painted scenes inspired by the French realists. He was the first professor and director of the Norwegian Academy of Arts from 1909–25. In 1889, he was made a knight in the French Legion of Honour and entered the Belgian Order of Leopold in 1894.

Peder Severin Krøyer
1851–1909, Norway
Realism, Impressionism
Peder Severin Krøyer (also referred to as P.S. Krøyer) was 14 years old when he enrolled at the Royal Academy of Fine Arts in Copenhagen. He was highly respected as a portrait painter and had many commissions. Krøyer helped Skagen grow as an artists' colony; he was fascinated with the town's life and portrayed the life of artists living there. He was adept at capturing dreamy gardens, the evening atmosphere and tranquil moonlit skies.

Sir John Lavery
1856–1941, Northern Ireland
Portraits
Sir John Lavery was best known for his society portraits and wartime depictions. His motivation to paint took him to Glasgow, where he tinted photographs to finance his art classes. There, Lavery befriended the artists known as the Glasgow Boys, with whom he shared an interest in subjects from modern life. He enjoyed great success after his move

to London in 1896, where he combined his talents as a portrait painter with an interest in contemporary events. Lavery was knighted in 1918.

Henri Lebasque
1865—1937, France
Post-Impressionism, Fauvism
Henri Lebasque spent most of his career painting in the south of France with his friends Pierre Bonnard, Édouard Vuillard and Henri Matisse. Critics praise him for the intimacy of his subject matter and the joy in his use of paint. His use of bold colours became more luminous and vibrant with time.

Richard E. Miller
1875—1943, America
American Impressionism, Giverny colony
Richard E. Miller was an eminent figurative painter whose work concentrated on women relaxing in gardens and interiors. He grew up in St Louis, Missouri, and finished his education at the Académie Julien in Paris. From 1906, he spent summers at the American artists' colony of Giverny, centred around Claude Monet's estate. When WWI broke out, he moved back to the US and settled in Pasadena, where he taught art.

Peder Mørk Mønsted
1859—1941, Denmark
Realism, Naturalism
Peder Mørk Mønsted began painting lessons at an early age and went on to study at the Royal Academy of Fine

Arts. In 1878, Mønsted studied under the artist Peder Severin Krøyer, who greatly influenced his style and practice. He began to develop a personal style of academic naturalism, paying great attention to light and detail. Mønsted was an ardent traveller and spent much time in Spain, Algeria, Greece and Switzerland.

Constant Montald
1862—1944, Belgium
Painter, muralist, sculptor, stained glass
Constant Montald studied at Ghent's technical school during the day, specialising in decorative arts, and at the Royal Academy of Fine Arts in the evening. He won a competition in 1885 and received a grant from the city, which enabled him to live and study briefly in Paris at the Beaux-Arts de Paris. Montald was fascinated by the repetitive patterns of trees, flowers and surreal growths, introducing musicality into his work.

Berthe Morisot
1841—1895, France
Impressionism
Berthe Morisot was the first woman to join the Impressionists. She was part of the first exhibition where the group called themselves 'impressionists' in 1877. Women of this period did not go to bars or cafés alone, therefore many of Morisot's subjects are in the home or garden. Although successful in her lifetime, being a female painter was still frowned upon and her work was not fully appreciated until years later.

Edvard Munch
1863–1944, Norway
Expressionism, Symbolism
Edvard Munch focused much of his creative agenda on the human condition, mortality, chronic illness, sexual liberation and religious aspiration. He seemingly extracted emotion from the subject through some portal, transcribing what he discovered onto canvas. His rich, effervescent colour palette is evident in much of his work.

Maxfield Parrish
1870–1966, America
Illustrator
Maxfield Parrish was a prolific illustrator and artist. He is noted for his distinctive saturated hues and idealised neo-classical imagery. His career spanned fifty years and was wildly successful. The National Museum of American Illustration deemed his painting *Daybreak* (1922) the most successful art print of the 20th century.

Eilif Peterssen
1852–1928, Norway
En plein air, Skagen School
Eilif Peterssen graduated from the Norwegian National Academy of Craft and Art Industry and completed his studies at the Royal Danish Academy of Fine Arts in Copenhagen. In 1905, he was commissioned to design the new coat of arms for Norway when they became independent from Sweden. Although he was known for his portraits, Peterssen enjoyed painting en plein air; mountains and scenery soon became his passion. After the death of his first wife, Nicoline, in 1882, Peterssen visited Skagen in Denmark together with a large group of artist friends. There, he painted some of his most evocative works.

Camille Pissarro
1830–1903, Denmark/France
Impressionism, Post-Impressionism
Camille Pissarro was born in St Thomas in what was the Danish West Indies, later attending boarding school in France. In 1855, he moved to Paris and became friends with Claude Monet, Paul Cézanne, Pierre-Auguste Renoir and Edgar Degas. Pissarro was the inventor of Impressionism and instrumental in the en plein air painting style. He was determined to pursue this technique even though his work proved unpopular.

Edward Henry Potthast
1857–1927, America
Impressionist, lithography, illustration
Edward Henry Potthast was born in Cincinnati, Ohio and studied art at the McMicken School. Potthast began work as a lithographer but moved on to study at the Royal Academy in Munich. Potthast worked as a magazine illustrator and exhibited regularly at the National Academy of Design. He is best remembered for his light-saturated paintings of Central Park, beaches and sweeping New England landscapes.

Dod Procter
1890–1972, Britain
Newlyn School
Dod Procter was born in London; her mother had studied at the Slade School

of Art. After her father's death, the family moved to Newlyn, Cornwall. Dod enrolled at the School of Painting, run by Elizabeth and Stanhope Forbes. She achieved success and her work was displayed at the Royal Academy. Dod was great friends with other artists in Cornwall, including Laura Knight and Alethea Garstin.

Hovsep Pushman
1878–1966, America/Armenia
Still lifes, Orientalism
Hovsep Pushman grew up in the Ottoman Empire, before emigrating to Chicago in 1896. Pushman studied Chinese culture and Asian art. He moved to Paris and studied at the Académie Julien; he received several medals and exhibited successfully. On his return to the US, he moved to California and co-founded the Laguna Beach Art Association with fellow painters. Many of his paintings are portraits of people, objects and artefacts of great metaphorical and symbolic significance.

Paul Ranson
1864–1909, France
Les Nabis, Symbolism
Paul Ranson was a painter and writer and also performed and directed plays. Fascinated by theosophy, magic and the occult, his paintings often depicted scenes full of mythology, witchcraft and anti-clerical subjects. His colour palette was opulent, adding to the feel of mystery.

Odilon Redon
1840–1916, France
Post-Impressionism, Symbolism
Odilon Redon fought in the Franco-Prussian War; he spent his spare time drawing in charcoal and making lithographs. After the war he moved on to pastels and oil paint. He was fascinated by different religions and cultures, and these themes became prominent in his work. His work was often described as a journey between dreams and nightmares as they contained fantastical figures and apparitions from his imagination.

Pierre-Auguste Renoir
1841–1919, France
Impressionism, Modern Art
Through his work, Pierre-Auguste Renoir celebrated beauty, especially feminine sensuality. It was said that 'Renoir is the final representative of a tradition which runs directly from Rubens to Watteau'.

Sir James Jebusa Shannon
1862–1923, America
Portraits
James Jebusa Shannon was born in New York and moved to Canada with his family. He studied painting in London during the 1880s and very quickly gained notoriety with his society portraits; he became a founding member of the Royal Society of Portrait Painters. Shannon was elected an associate of the Royal Academy of Art and, in 1922, renounced his United States' citizenship in order to accept a knighthood.

Hugo Simberg
1873—1917, Finland
Symbolism
Hugo Simberg attended the Vyborg Drawing School for Art Lovers and later studied at the Finnish Art Society Art School in Helsinki; his teacher was Helena Schjerfbeck. He decided to withdraw from the art school and approached the painter Akseli Gallen-Kallela for lessons. After several successful exhibitions, Simberg was accepted into the Union of Artists of Finland. Many of his paintings and drawings depict morbid scenes, life and death, angels and devils.

Harald Slott-Møller
1864—1937, Denmark
Ceramicist, Symbolism
In 1883, Harald Slott-Møller completed a foundation course at the Royal Danish Academy of Fine Arts. Slott-Møller then painted for three years under Peder Severin Krøyer's tutorship. Slott-Møller and his wife, the artist Agnes Slott-Møller (née Rambusch), were founding members of Den Frie Udstilling, 'The Free Exhibition'. The couple both enjoyed Italian art and the allegorical themes of the Pre-Raphaelites. Slott-Møller became a Knight of the Dannebrog in 1919.

Harald Oskar Sohlberg
1869—1935, Norway
Neo-romanticism, Modernism, Symbolism, Realism
Harald Oskar Sohlberg sought inspiration from local scenes where he captured the ever-changing northern light. His unique colour palette and tonal range impressed his contemporaries. His work captures an air of mystery and magic, tempting the viewer out beyond the horizon.

Thure Sundell
1864-1924, Finland
Realism
Thure Sundell secured a scholarship to study at the Royal Stockholm Academy. Many of his friends went on to Paris, but he preferred a peaceful and rural life. Sundell lived like a hermit and found an affinity for a small island called Kaskinen. Here, he immersed himself in the simple life of the sea and shoreline. His friends tried to coax him out of his solitude; occasionally, he'd enter competitions and often won. But publicity wasn't for him; he believed it was wrong to charge for his paintings, so he took small sums, meaning he lived most of his life in poverty. Tragically, in 1924, a year after inheriting a large amount of money, he died of skin cancer.

José Tapiró y Baró
1836—1913, Spain
Orientalism
José Tapiró y Baró showed talent in art from a young age. He took lessons with a local wine merchant and amateur painter, Domènec Soberano. He was primarily taught about historical and religious subjects, closely associated with the Nazarene movement. In 1871, he travelled to Tangier, which marked the beginning of his love with Orientalism. He eventually moved to Tangier in 1876.

Ellen Thesleff
1869–1954, Finland
Expressionism, Modernism, Symbolism

Ellen Thesleff was the eldest of five siblings. Thesleff's father was an amateur painter, and the family were musical; Thesleff sang and played piano. At sixteen, she enrolled in Adolf von Becker's private painting academy and studied with fellow students Helene Schjerfbeck and Akseli Gallen-Kallela. Thesleff completed her training in Paris and in 1891 enrolled at the Académie Colarossi. She later travelled to Florence, learned about the Renaissance, and met Gordon Craig, who introduced her to the technique of wood engraving.

Gaston La Touche
1854–1896, France
Illustrator, engraver, sculptor,
Symbolism, Impressionism

Gaston La Touche (or Gaston de La Touche) showed a talent for art from a young age. He received lessons from a local tutor, but had to seek refuge with his family in Normandy at the start of the Franco-Prussian War. He had no further training. However, he exhibited widely and became friends with Edgar Degas and Édouard Manet and collaborated with Émile Zola by illustrating *L'Assommoir* and other works. La Touche won several medals for his work, including the Gold Medal at the Exposition Universelle in Paris in 1900.

Henry Scott Tuke
1858–1929, Britain
Newlyn School, Impressionism

Henry Scott Tuke was primarily a painter and a photographer and is best known for his paintings of bathing scenes. During the 1880s, Tuke met Oscar Wilde, John Addington Symonds and many other poetic luminaries. Tuke wrote a 'Sonnet to Youth', published anonymously in *The Artist* magazine. Often painting in the open air, he went against fashion, favouring immediate, strong brush strokes rather than the more popular slick finish.

Suzanne Valadon
1865–1938, France
Post-Impressionism, Symbolism

Suzanne Valadon grew up in poverty and only attended school until she was eleven. At fifteen, she joined the circus as an acrobat, but injured her spine in a fall. Despite her upbringing, Valadon was the first female painter to be admitted to the Société Nationale des Beaux-Arts. She was also the mother of painter Maurice Utrillo. Valadon painted female nudes, still lifes and landscapes, and shocked her male colleagues by painting unflattering portraits of men. She was Henri de Toulouse-Lautrec's lover, an affair which ended after two years when she tried to commit suicide. She later married Paul Mousis, a wealthy stockbroker and was able to paint full-time, but the marriage ended when she began an affair with André Utter, a twenty-three-year-old friend of her son. Utter modelled for her, and they later married, often exhibiting their work together.

Félix Vallotton
1865—1925, Switzerland/France
Les Nabis, printmaking, woodcuts
Félix Vallotton was an essential figure in the development of the modern woodcut. He painted portraits, landscapes, nudes, still lifes and other subjects in an unemotional, realistic style. His vibrant use of colour defined his paintings. By contrast, his prints are characterised by broad masses of black and white with minimal detail.

John William Waterhouse
1849—1917, Britain
Academic Style, Pre-Raphaelite
John William Waterhouse began working in the Academic Style and later embraced the Pre-Raphaelite Brotherhood's ethos. He is remembered for his intricate detail and depiction of women from ancient Greek Mythology, Arthurian Legend and poetry. Each of his paintings brims with allegory and narrative.

Jens Ferdinand Willumsen
1863—1958, Denmark
Symbolism, Expressionism, Skagen Painters, photography, sculptor, architecture, ceramics
Jens Ferdinand Willumsen attended the Royal Danish Academy of Fine Arts and the Copenhagen Technical College. He majored in fine art and architecture and studied under P.S. Krøyer and Laurits Tuxen. Willumsen visited Norway in 1892 and became closely linked with the Skagen painters. Willumsen travelled throughout Europe and lived almost half his life in France, where he settled.

Leon Wyczółkowski
1852—1936, Poland
Young Poland movement, Realism, the Interbellum, Symbolism, Impressionism
Leon Wyczółkowski was an influential Polish painter. From 1895 to 1911, he was a professor at the Jan Matejko Academy of Fine Art in Kraków and Warsaw. He was also a founding member of the Society of Polish Artists. Wyczółkowski began by implementing documentary realism, but after a visit to Paris, he was seduced by the techniques of the French Impressionists.

Artwork locations

Lawrence Alma-Tadema, The Favourite Poet, 1888. *Lady Lever Art Gallery, Wirral, UK.*

Lawrence Alma-Tadema, In a Rose Garden. *Private collection.*

Michael Ancher, Promenade on the Beach. *Skagens Museum, Denmark.*

Anders Andersen-Lundby, A Winter Day with Trees Illuminated by the Sunset, 1887–97. *Not on display.*

Nikolai Astrup, Foxgloves, woodblock c.1915–20; print 1925. *Private collection.*

Nikolai Astrup, March Morning, Spring Night and Willow. *Private collection.*

Firmin Baes, The Dream of the Lacemaker. *Private collection.*

Marie Bashkirtseff, The Umbrella, 1883. *State Russian Museum, St. Petersburg, Russia.*

Jules Bastien-Lepage, Le Père Jacques (The Wood Gatherer), 1881. *Milwaukee Art Museum, Wisconsin, USA.*

Jules Bastien-Lepage, Rural Love, 1882. *Pushkin Museum, Moscow, Russia.*

Marie-Guillemine Benoist, Portrait of Madeleine, 1799–1800. *Musée du Louvre, Paris, France.*

Lamorna Birch, The Dipper's Playground, 1948. *Private collection.*

Edwin Howland Blashfield, Spring Scattered Stars, 1927. *Private collection.*

Pierre Bonnard, The Garden under the Snow, Sunset, c.1910. *Private collection.*

Pierre Bonnard, Nude in Backlighting, or The Eau de Cologne, 1908–09. *Musée d'Art Moderne, Brussels, Belgium.*

Frank Bramley, Eyes and No Eyes, 1887. *Penlee House Gallery and Museum, Penzance, UK.*

Franklin Carmichael, Autumn Hillside, 1920. *Art Gallery of Ontario, Canada.*

Marc Chagall, Bouquet with Flying Lovers, c.1934–47. *Private collection.*

Emile Claus, Sunset over Waterloo Bridge, 1916. *Gallery Oscar De Vos, Belgium.*

George Clausen, The Little Flowers of the Field, 1895. *Private collection.*

Frank Dicksee, On the Brittany Coast. *The Maas Gallery, London, UK.*

Frank Dicksee, The Sensitive Plant. *Private collection.*

Nikolay Nikanorovich Dubovskoy, It Grew Quiet, 1890. *State Russian Museum, St Petersburg, Russia.*

František Dvořák, The Angel of the Birds, 1910. *Dahesh Museum of Art, New York, USA.*

Janet Fisher, Distant Thoughts. *Private collection.*

Gustaf Fjæstad, Frost in Sunshine, 1921. *Private collection.*

Frederick Carl Frieseke, Lady in a Garden, c.1912. *Terra Foundation of American Art, Chicago, IL, USA.*

Akseli Gallen-Kallela, Lake Keitele, 1905. *National Gallery, London, UK.*

William Fraser Garden, A Great Tree on a Riverbank, 1892. *Private collection.*

Eva Gonzalès, Woman Awakening, 1876. *Guggenheim Museum Bilbao, Spain.*

Pekka Halonen, Woman in Boat, 1924. *Ateneum Art Museum, Finnish National Gallery, Helsinki, Finland.*

Angus Hampel, Hope, 2015. *Private collection.*

Edwin Harris, Sweet Dreams, 1892. *Private collection.*

Childe Hassam, Rain Storm, Union Square, 1890. *Museum of the City of New York, USA.*

Olga Kurtz Hasselmann, Josephine Baker, c.1930. *Private collection.*

George Henry, Japanese Lady with a Fan, 1894. *Art Gallery and Museum, Kelvingrove, Glasgow, Scotland.*

George Henry and Edward Atkinson Hornel, The Druids: Bringing in the Mistletoe, 1890. *Art Gallery and Museum, Kelvingrove, Glasgow, Scotland.*

Utagawa Hiroshige, New Year's Eve Foxfires at the Changing Tree, Ōji, c.1857. *Not on display.*

Carl Holsøe, A Woman Seated at a Table by a Window, c.1900. *Private collection.*

Winslow Homer, A Summer Night, 1890. *Musée d'Orsay, Paris, France.*

Edward Atkinson Hornel, Tom-Tom Players, Ceylon, 1908. *Private collection.*

Edward Robert Hughes, Twilight Fantasies, 1911. *Private collection.*

Peter Ilsted, The Open Door, 1912. *Private collection.*

Augustus John, Head of a Jamaican Girl, c.1937. *Private collection.*

Gustav Klimt, Island in the Attersee, 1902. *Private collection.*

Laura Knight, Lamorna Cove, c.1912. *Private collection.*

Christian Krohg, Little Ebbe Reading, 1920. *Private collection.*

Christian Krohg, Oda with Lamp. *Private collection.*

Peder Severin Krøyer, Hip Hip Hurrah! Artists' Party at Skagen, 1888. *Gothenburg Museum of Art, Gothenburg, Sweden.*

Peder Severin Krøyer, Summer Evening at Skagen, the Artist's Wife with a Dog on the Beach, 1892. *Skagens Museum, Denmark.*

John Lavery, Anna Pavlova, 1910. *Art Gallery and Museum, Kelvingrove, Glasgow, Scotland.*

Henri Lebasque, Girl Reading. *Musée Marmottan Monet, Paris, France.*

Richard E. Miller, Afternoon Tea, 1910. *Indianapolis Museum of Art at Newfields, USA.*

Peder Mørk Mønsted, An Old Woman Knitting at the Window, 1929. *Not on display.*

Constant Montald, Dancing Nymphs, 1898. *Fin-de-Siècle Museum, Brussels, Belgium.*

Berthe Morisot, The Cherry Picker, 1891. *Private collection.*

Edvard Munch, The Kiss, 1897. *National Museum, Oslo, Norway.*

Maxfield Parrish, Ecstasy, 1929. *National Museum of American Illustration & American Illustrators Gallery, Newport, RI, USA.*

Eilif Peterssen, Nocturne, 1887. *National Museum, Stockholm, Sweden.*

Camille Pissarro, Road Climbing to Osny, 1883. *Musée des Beaux-Arts, Valenciennes, France.*

Edward Henry Potthast, Dutch Interior, 1890. *Cincinnati Art Museum, Ohio, USA.*

Dod Procter, Gabriel in St Lucia, c.1950s. *Penlee House Gallery and Museum, Penzance, Cornwall, UK.*

Hovsep Pushman, The Incense Burner, c.1919. *Not on display.*

Paul Ranson, The Blue or Nude Room at the Fan, 1891. *Private collection.*

Odilon Redon, Ophelia among the Flowers, 1905–08. *Royal Academy of Arts, London, UK.*

Pierre-Auguste Renoir, Confidence, 1897. *Private collection.*

James Jebusa Shannon, The Purple Stocking. *South African National Gallery, Cape Town, South Africa.*

Hugo Simberg, Towards the Evening, 1913. *Finnish National Gallery, Helsinki, Finland.*

Harald Slott-Møller, Midsummer's Eve, 1904. *Not on display.*

Harald Oskar Sohlberg, Winter Nights in the Mountains, 1914. *Private collection.*

Thure Sundell, Moonlight. *Not on display.*

José Tapiró y Baró, A Tangerian Beauty, c.1876. *Dahesh Museum of Art, New York, USA.*

Ellen Thesleff, Echo, 1891. *Private collection.*

Gaston La Touche, Lovers and Swans; The Autumn Walk, 1896. *Private collection.*

Henry Scott Tuke, The Critics, 1927. *Leamington Spa Art Gallery & Museum, UK.*

Suzanne Valadon, Bouquet and a Cat, 1919. *Private collection.*

Félix Vallotton, The Library, 1921. *Musée Maurice Denis, St. Germain-en-Laye, France.*

Félix Vallotton, Martiniquaise, 1915. *Private collection.*

John William Waterhouse, A Mermaid, 1900. *Royal Academy of Arts, London, UK.*

John William Waterhouse, Soul of the Rose, 1908. *Private collection.*

Jens Ferdinand Willumsen, Young Woman Walking in the Mountains, 1904. *Private collection.*

Leon Wyczółkowski, Gościeradza, 1933. *Not on display.*

Index of artists

Index of writers

General index

Picture credits

Acknowledgements

Henry Beston, *The Outermost House*, copyright © The Estate of Henry Beston, Macmillan.

Excerpt(s) from WINTERING: THE POWER OF REST AND RETREAT IN DIFFICULT TIMES by Katherine May, copyright © 2020 by Katherine May. Used by permission of Riverhead, an imprint of Penguin Publishing Group, a division of Penguin Random House LLC. All rights reserved.

Vita Sackville-West, *The Land*, copyright © The Estate of Vita Sackville-West.

Helen Keller, from *My Key of Life (Optimism)*. Reproduced by permission of the Helen Keller Archives.

Iain Thomas, *I Wrote This For You*, copyright © Iain Thomas.

The Four Loves by C.S. Lewis copyright © 1960 C.S. Lewis Pte. Ltd. Extract reprinted by permission.

Willa Cather, from *O Pioneers!*. Reproduced by permission of the Willa Cather Trust.

Haruki Murakami, *Kafka on the Shore*, copyright © Haruki Murakami, 2002, Penguin Random House.

Wendy Lustbader, from *Life Gets Better: The Unexpected Pleasures of Growing Older*. Reproduced by permission of Dystel, Goderich & Bourret LLC.

W.S. Merwin, 'To Paula in Late Spring' from *The Shadow of Sirius*, copyright © The Estate of W.S. Merwin, 2009, Copper Canyon Press.

"Phenomenal Woman" from AND STILL I RISE: A BOOK OF POEMS by Maya Angelou, copyright © 1978 by Caged Bird Legacy, LLC. Used by permission of Random House, an imprint and division of Penguin Random House LLC. All rights reserved.

E.M. Forster, *A Room with a View*, copyright © The Estate of E.M. Forster, 1908, Penguin Classics.

Ram Dass quote on page 92 reproduced by permission of the author. For more information go to ramdass.org.

Louise Erdrich, *The Painted Drum*, copyright © Louise Erdrich, 2005.

Nora Ephron quote on page 113 copyright © Heartburn Enterprises, Inc., 2006. Reprinted by permission of Heartburn Enterprises, Inc.

Aldous Huxley, from *Point Counter Point*. Reproduced by permission of Dalkey Archive Press.

Brian Jacques, *The Taggerung*, copyright © The Estate of Brian Jacques, 2001, Penguin Random House.

Robert Brault quote on page 142 reproduced by permission of the author, Robert Brault, American Writer, 1938–

"Evidence" by Mary Oliver
Reprinted by the permission of The Charlotte Sheedy Literary Agency as agent for the author. Copyright © 2009, 2017 by Mary Oliver with permission of Bill Reichblum.

From ONE HUNDRED LOVE SONNETS: CIEN SONETOS DE AMOR by Pablo Neruda, translated by Stephen Tapscott, Copyright © Pablo Neruda 1959 and Fundación Pablo Neruda, Copyright © 1986 by the University of Texas Press. By permission of the University of Texas Press.

Mark Strand, *The Late Hour*, © The Estate of Mark Strand, 1978.

'The Dream Keeper' by Langston Hughes from *The Collected Poems of Langston Hughes* (Alfred A Knopf Inc), reproduced by permission of David Higham Associates Limited.

Batsford is committed to respecting the intellectual property rights of others. We have taken all reasonable efforts to ensure that the reproduction of all contents on these pages is done with the full consent of the copyright owners. If you are aware of unintentional omissions, please contact the company directly so that any necessary corrections may be made for future editions.

'I was a late bloomer. But anyone who blooms at all, ever, is very lucky.'

Sharon Olds, poet

This book is dedicated to my therapist, Catherine, my eclectic friends and neighbours who have supported and inspired me on this rollercoaster of life. A huge shout out to Pandora, Nic, Pete, Youth, Maryann, Jo, Jane, Rufus, Chez, Rob and the rest of you, you know who you are!

Oliver-Bizhan, Caspian and Anousheh, I love you always.